anythink

WOULD YOU DARE?

WOULD YOU DARE RUN A MARATHON?

By Siobhan Sisk

Gareth Stevens
PUBLISHING

Please visit our website, www.garethstevens.com. For a free color catalog of all our high-quality books, call toll free 1-800-542-2595 or fax 1-877-542-2596.

Library of Congress Cataloging-in-Publication Data

Names: Sisk, Siobhan, author.
Title: Would you dare run a marathon? / Siobhan Sisk.
Description: New York : Gareth Stevens Publishing, [2017] | Series: Would you dare? | Includes index.
Identifiers: LCCN 2016031625| ISBN 9781482458220 (Paperback Book) | ISBN 9781482458237 (6 pack) | ISBN 9781482458244 (Library Bound Book)
Subjects: LCSH: Marathon running--Juvenile literature. | Marathon running--History--Juvenile literature.
Classification: LCC GV1065 .S57 2017 | DDC 796.42/52--dc23
LC record available at https://lccn.loc.gov/2016031625

First Edition

Published in 2017 by
Gareth Stevens Publishing
111 East 14th Street, Suite 349
New York, NY 10003

Designer: Laura Bowen
Editor: Therese Shea

Photo credits: Cover, p. 1 (runner) THOMAS SAMSON/AFP/Getty Images; cover, p. 1 (crowd) Francis Tsang/Cover/Getty Images; cover, pp. 1–32 (background) Nik Merkulov/Shutterstock.com; cover, pp. 1–32 (paint splat) Milan M/Shutterstock.com; cover, pp. 1–32 (photo frame) Milos Djapovic/Shutterstock.com; p. 5 Joseph Sohm/ Shutterstock.com; p. 6 Shane White/Shutterstock.com; p. 7 Daniel Korzeniewski/ Shutterstock.com; pp. 8, 30 FCG/Shutterstock.com; p. 9 Marcio Jose Bastos Silva/ Shutterstock.com; p. 11 mimagephotography/Shutterstock.com; p. 13 Maridav/ Shutterstock.com; p. 15 Daxiao Productions/Shutterstock.com; p. 17 antoniodiaz/ Shutterstock.com; p. 19 Marko Rupena/Shutterstock.com; p. 21 Suzan Oschmann/ Shutterstock.com; p. 22 JTang/Shutterstock.com; p. 23 Maddie Meyer/Getty Images Sport/ Getty Images; p. 24 Rena Schild/Shutterstock.com; p. 25 David Madison/The Image Bank/ Getty Images; p. 27 Ashley Cooper/Corbis Documentary/Getty Images; p. 29 Jonathan Daniel/Getty Images Sport/Getty Images.

Printed in China

CPSIA compliance information: Batch #CW17GS: For further information contact Gareth Stevens, New York, New York at 1-800-542-2595.

CONTENTS

READY TO RUN?

You likely run every day. Maybe you run to the bus or to the dinner table. But can you imagine running for 26.2 miles (42.2 km)? That's the length of a marathon. Read on to find out more about this hard race!

DARING DATA

About 0.5 percent of the US population has run a marathon.

5

People want to run marathons for different reasons. Some want to get fit or lose weight. Others run marathons to raise money for causes. Still others just want a **challenge**. They want to prove to themselves that they can do it.

DARING DATA

Running makes your heart stronger, improves blood flow, and strengthens **muscles**.

You need to train a long time to run the length of a marathon. Not many people would have the **endurance** to run that long without training. Even fewer could run it and finish with a **competitive** time.

DARING DATA

In 2015, there were about 1,100 marathons in the United States.

TIME TO
TRAIN

Many trainers suggest running for a year before trying a marathon. They say to run about four times a week and slowly make the runs longer and longer. Running too long too quickly may lead to injury, or harm.

DARING DATA

Resting your body is just as important as running, so body parts can mend and become stronger.

Many training plans include at least one run a week that's longer than the others. That, too, lengthens each week. However, many running coaches think going the whole marathon **distance** before the real event raises the chance of injury.

DARING DATA

The long run each training week helps prepare your body for the marathon.

13

Besides increasing distance, training workouts may include speed runs. This means running faster than your usual **pace**. Speed runs help you if you want to finish the race in a shorter time. They also help build endurance.

DARING DATA

An interval run is made up of different paces. You start out running slow, then speed up. You do this over and over. It's a way to build speed.

15

MARATHON MEALS

Food and drink are also important parts of training. You need to eat to have the energy, or power, to run. It's best to eat a few hours before you run. It's also important to eat after your run for your body to **recover** faster.

DARING DATA

Some people eat while they're running, too!

It's important to drink enough water while marathon training. You should drink before you run. If you're running for more than 45 minutes, you should drink a bit about every 15 minutes. Sports drinks contain salt that helps with recovery.

DARING DATA

You sweat more in warm weather, so it's important to drink even more water when running.

FAMOUS MARATHONS

The first New York City Marathon, in 1970, had only 55 finishers out of 127 runners. Today, it's the largest marathon in the world. In 2015, a total of 49,595 runners finished. They were from 129 countries and all 50 states!

DARING DATA

The oldest person to complete the New York City Marathon was 93!

Not every marathon accepts all runners. You'll need to **qualify** for certain marathons. They may require that runners have completed a marathon in a certain time, such as under 4 hours. The Boston Marathon is one of the hardest to qualify for.

DARING DATA

The first-place men and women in the
Boston Marathon are given $150,000 each!

Not all marathons are the same. Some, such as the San Francisco Marathon, have challenging hills. The Marine Corps Marathon takes runners by famous monuments in Washington, DC. Many cities put on a Rock 'n' Roll Marathon. Bands play along the way!

Marine Corps Marathon

DARING DATA

The San Francisco Marathon is called
the "race even marathoners fear."

ULTRAMARATHONS

If 26.2 miles (42.2 km) isn't challenging enough, you could run an ultramarathon! That's any running event longer than a marathon. Some are as long as 100 miles (161 km)! There are often places along the way for runners to rest.

DARING DATA

Some ultramarathoners say they have hallucinations while running—they see things that aren't there!

ARE YOU
READY?

Many marathons require runners to be at least 18 years old. Young runners can prepare for future marathons by running short races. Just remember: you don't have to be first across the finish line to be a winner! So, would you dare be a marathoner?

DARING DATA

About 1 million people line the path of the Chicago Marathon each year. Cheer on the runners of the marathon near you!

Chicago
Marathon

29

MARATHON NUMBERS

To complete a marathon, you'd have to:

- walk about **45,000** steps

- climb Mount Everest **4.7** times

- climb the stairs of Burj Khalifa, the tallest building in the world, **19** times

- run the length of a football field **42** times

- run around a baseball diamond **384** times

FOR MORE INFORMATION

BOOKS

Birmingham, Maria. *Weird Zone: Sports*. Toronto, ON, Canada: Owlkids Books, 2013.

Wiseman, Blaine. *Boston Marathon*. New York, NY: Weigl Publishing Inc., 2011.

Yakin, Boaz, and Joe Infurnari. *Marathon*. New York, NY: First Second, 2012.

WEBSITES

Kids and Exercise
kidshealth.org/en/parents/exercise.html
Read how running and other exercise affects the body.

TCS Runfographics
www.tcsnycmarathon.org/tcs-runfographics
Read and watch some interesting info about the New York City Marathon and others.

GLOSSARY

challenge: something that is hard to do

competitive: having a wish to win or be the best at something

distance: the length between two things

endurance: the ability to do something hard for a long time

muscle: a part of the body that allows movement

pace: the speed at which someone moves

qualify: to have the skills to do a job or activity

recover: to return to everyday health

INDEX